The African OmniDevelopment Space Complex

The African OmniDevelopment Space Complex

Ra'maat Ubadah Hotep Ankh McConner Iheru

New York

The African Omnidevelopment Space Complex / We New
Copyright ©2022 All rights reserved.

Performance photo by Ricky Loew.
Ubadah McConner - bass,
Fareed (Harvey) McKnight - flute.

Handwritten correspondence
excerpt from Ubadah McConner.

Poster collages by Ubadah McConner created for the
African Omnidevelopment Space Complex / We New.

Thanks to Ubadah McConner Jr., Harvey McKnight,
Michael Carey and all who supported
and participated in the African
Omnidevelopment Space Complex / We New.

Cover design · Arteidolia Press

ARTEIDOLIA PRESS
P.O. Box 157
New York, N.Y. 10276

www.arteidolia.com/arteidolia-press

First Edition
Library of Congress Control Number: 2022905420
ISBN: 978-1-7369983-4-2

my A Game
backed by SQUABBING, SCRUMMING,
GRINDING AND GRINDHOUSE RE
INVENTION OF MY WE NEW
SELF, TO RE SCULPTURE
MY OWN DESTINY

Introduction by Michael Carey

Writing Black Out Loud 1939-1959 . . . 1

Bloomfield Hills 1952-1959 . . . 6

Air Force 1959-1963 . . . 16

Pontiac 1963-1972 . . . 26

The African Omnidevelopment . . . 39
Space Complex / We New

My Pontiac Motors Family . . . 58

On from the 70s into 2002 . . . 62

Afterword by patrick brennan . . . 68

Introduction

Art is the barometer and the forecast of the condition of a society.

I met Ubadah in 1969-1970.

The early '70s post riot period, the politically charged Vietnam War era, Mohammed Ali refusing the draft and prison time, Nixon and the politics that went with it were some but not all of the factors that went into an artistic renaissance and birth of a new hunger for knowledge and growth in self awareness and Blackman's culture and heritage. While American cities were on fire with hate, some of us saw our chance to go to college and advance our cause for equality through education [Affirmative action]. Our meetings every Friday for over 30 years at Ubadah's house involved all of the above and more.

Had those Friday sessions not taken place, I am certain that I would have continued with the help of other higher caliber artists who nurtured me to personally develop myself as the professional musician challenge because in this music, we all learned at different rates and all shared the growth and interaction and over the years a matriculation took place. It was a think tank of sorts where each person contributed and each contributor reaped knowledge in return.

Some fell by the wayside as some always do, and some players took their knowledge into other fields. A Detroit visiting sax player named Shaney later became a doctor. I went into engineering and worked for G.M. Proving Grounds for 35 years. Others went into law practice and so on.

This was an Artistic and cultural haven and sanctuary for those who searched for self understanding through challenging times. Ubadah extended his hospitality to all who came with true hearts.

NOTE!!! in all the 38 years of these Friday night, all night sessions, there were NEVER any fights, unruliness, no upset neighbors, no police visits.

That's a sign of great respect from everyone to Ubadah.

- Michael Carey

Writing Black Out Loud

1939-1959

Saturday, November 11, 1939, sixteen minutes after high noon, at precisely 12:16 pm, I came into this existence on the Southside of Pontiac, Michigan 30 minutes after the birth of my twin brother Rashid. In fact, I was born and raised in a house just a driveway distance away from the community's legendary after hours joint that went from all night Friday night until all night Saturday. Sunday was for church and Monday was Blue Monday.

When Rashid and I were delivered in the house at 517 Harvey, we were delivered right into the music that was still vibrating and incessantly pumping out every blues record recorded at that time. From November 11, 1939 to June 12, 1951, when my family was living next door to Georgie Manning, I was fortunate to have listened to all the great Blues, Rhythm and Blues and Black Music in that epoch of my childhood. The bed that I slept in for my first 12 years was right in the center of all the music that boomed and blasted out of the basement windows and door.

Mrs. Georgie loved music, and she had literally hundreds of records stacked all up in piles. I remember so vividly because I began my record collection based on my memory of hers. So, when I research my history and memory, this basement music studio sonic boom sound was my first lasting impression. Rashid and I had Friday night music concerts all during these hot summer months. That music was drummed into me.

Here is a list of some of the blues musicians that I remember hearing and growing up with during my first 12 years — Little Walter, B.B. King, Ray Milton, T-Bone Walker, Big Joe Turner, Amos Milburn, Memphis Slim, Muddy Waters, John Lee Hooker, Albert King. Sonny Boy Williamson, Howling Wolf — and then there was the Pontiac Southside legendary Blues piano player, the fabled Earlie B.

In that basement surrounded by tables weighed down with stacks and stacks of records was an old Black piano. Late, late in the wee hours of those hot summer and cold, frigid winter nights, Earlie B. would come out of his Friday night drinking binge and become a glowing red hot piece of Black cool and set that piano on so much fire that it would heat up that basement room until it rocked nonstop like a roaring train. In the summertime, I lay there in my bed at a concert, and I loved to let the music sweep me away in its totality. In the winter, the piano and all the rocking going on seemed to make the windows glow, throb, and the power in that basement, the music that empowered and nurtured me those first 12 years of my life was a very spiritual experience that has remained with me all the days of my life. I credit Mrs. Georgie and Earlie B. as my first two music professors, and when I explore my music roots and my love and involvement in history and memory. I am proud and glad to call them my first musical beginning.

After we departed from our first music learning scene, my mother, Virginia McConner, took over, and her love of music was so complete and dramatic that she introduced me and Rashid first hand to Miles, Bird, Yusef Lateef, Horace Silver, Art Blakey, Duke Ellington, Dinah Washington, Sarah Vaughn, Ella Fitzgerald, The Clara Ward Singers, the Platters, all the popular rhythm and blues records, James Brown, Ray Charles, Count Basie, The Midnighters, The Moonglows; and in 1951, when we first moved into our new family home at 1421 Franklin Road, in Bloomfield Hills, Michigan I was allowed to cultivate my burgeoning love for music under the tutelage of my mother.

Rashid and I owe our love for jazz music to my mother's love for jazz music. She introduced us to Thelonious Monk with his Riverside record, Brilliant Corners, and she also gave us the music of Charles

Mingus with his record Pithecanthropus Erectus. Then, she introduced me to Paul Lawrence Dunbar Chambers when she received Round About Midnight in her 1958 selection from her Columbia Record Club membership. I remember that day in the 1958 summer like it was yesterday morning. I opened up the package with the record and put it on the record player and walked away, and before I had gone 3 or 4 feet, the power of Paul Chambers grabbed me with an understanding that I wanted to play the bass. It was that instant moment that life reinvented itself in me.

BLOOMFIELD HILLS

1952-1959

But — however — let me back up to 1952 again because suddenly my family house was no longer in the heart of the Pontiac Black gritty ghetto neighborhood, but now a block outside of the Pontiac city limits in an all white neighborhood in Bloomfield Hills — and my family was the only Black family in that white community.

I was 12 years old and in the prime of my childhood innocence and trust. So I was not looking at color. I was beyond color, being so young, and when I first hit the streets of my new neighborhood, a battalion of white children were waiting on me and Rashid to welcome us into their families.

They are still my families to this day, and I could not have become who I am today without their love, support, loyal protection and their faith in me.

I have never been a racist and, even though this was during the time of residential covenants, of all white city governments, police forces, fire departments, invisible racial boundary lines and socially taboo interactions with white traditions, I'd already grown up for 12 years in a white and Black neighborhood in the south side of Pontiac with white brothers I'd grown from the cradle with. We were actually brothers from the cradle, to kindergarden through elementary school and three years of Junior High School.

NOW — when I say we were like brothers, that truth honors who I am today. I never heard the word "nigger" from anybody. I ran in and out of my brothers' houses, spent the night with them, ate with them, knew their daddies and mamas, giving me a sense of myself in Pontiac that was very sensible and enduring.

My mother was strictly an at-home homemaker, and she watched over all of us on the street like a mother hen. Just as significant – when I was 12 she filled the house with music morning, noon and night, and when I got up in the morning she had the coffee and the radio on. She cleaned house by music, cooked daily by music, washed and ironed clothes by music, visited with her company by music, taught us how to dance with her music, and whenever she had one of her many card playing house parties, music was served far into the night. I lay in my bed many nights, mornings and was serenaded by all the wonderful music my mother played from her growing record collection in 1952, 1953, 1954, 1955, 1956 and 1958.

Then there were Rashid's musical discoveries that he brought home in the form of the latest doo-wop, rhythm and blues, rock and roll and early jazz 78s. Rashid was much, much more outgoing, adventurous, ambitious, fearless, curious, aggressive and advanced during our early and late adolescence. He was always out exploring, and I was always waiting on his new discoveries.

In 1955, when we were 15, he brought home a stack of 78s by Charlie Parker and Miles Davis that were the famous Dial record series. That was my very first exposure to bebop, Bird and Miles Davis — and after we listened to that particular collection of records, we became full fledged jazz music hard core relentless devotees. Jazz music became our life; and it was during those 1955 times that we earnestly began our jazz record devotion and our fanatic love for Downbeat magazine.

Like I said, our mother's record collection was very important because, as our love of jazz grew, she started buying a lot of jazz records that exposed us more and more to all the important jazz musicians of the early and late 1950s. My mother had beautiful taste, and it was she who brought the records we really needed to hear and brought to us the great jazz musicians who were our heroes and champions. When Rashid and I played music, we played the jazz records our mother had brought and when we went places we always had some jazz records with us and soon we became known for our love for jazz.

Now, this was 1955, 1956, 1957 — whenever we got up 5 or 6 dollars we (Rashid and I) raced full throttle to Art's Record Store in downtown Pontiac to purchase an album, and then we raced full throttle back home to listen to it. That was our life and we loved it. We listened to our growing record collection every day after school, all day on Saturday and Sunday, and the more we listened, the more music became the pivotal center of our existence.

When I turned 16, I met my first girlfriend, who is now my wife – Gloria Ann Gamble, the niece of Hank, Thad, Elvin, Paul, Lynn Thomas, and Anna Mae Jones. When I met her in September 1956, she was 14 and I had no idea that she had been raised in the same house that Elvin Jones had lived in or that she had been a child when he had lived there. She was there when Elvin Jones had his famous Monday night jam sessions that Paul Chambers, Doug Watkins, Barry Harris, Milt Jackson, Bess Bonnier, the McKinney brothers, Pepper Adams, Kenny Burrell and even Miles

Davis and countless other Detroit musicians came out to Pontiac to attend.

Music was everything, and we spent hours, and hours and hours listening to music just as we still do to this day. At that time I was heavily into Horace Silver, Art Blakey's Jazz Messengers, Yusef Lateef, Charles Mingus, Monk, Lee Morgan, Miles Davis, Sonny Rollins, Coltrane, Max Roach — and I was either at home listening to those musicians or listening at her house.

It is important to me in the power of my history and memory that I reflect on the jazz records Rashid and I attained from 1955 to 1958. These particular records were our most prized and precious possessions because they possessed all of our waking moments trying to satisfy our voracious hunger at the ages of 15, 16 and 17. The years 1955, 1956 and 1957 were centered around the music we listened to mainly because these were the records we had attained.

We had Miles Davis' small 33 record on Prestige with Blue Haze, Solar, A Night in Tunisia, and Yusef Lateef's Savoy album, Morning, Art Blakey's Hard Bop and Dream Suite, Charles Mingus' Pithecanthropus Erectus, Frank Wess' Flutes and Reeds, Duke Ellington at Newport 1956, Art Blakey Jazz Messengers' Hard Drive, The Jazz Messengers on Blue Note with Horace

Silver, Doug Watkins, Kenny Dorham and Art Blakey, Art Blakey and the Jazz Messengers, Midnight Night Session; and I can recall vividly each album that we purchased and how they became the utmost center of our undivided rapt attention.

One Saturday, we marched down to Art's Record Store in an army of four or five of us and we copped Jackie McLean and Company with Jackie McLean, Bill Hardman, Mal Waldron, Doug Watkins, Art Taylor and Ray Draper on Tuba. When we got that album home we almost literally climbed into that music and lived it, breathed it, sang it and it became a mantra of existence that kept us fascinated. Just having Ray Draper's tuba with Jackie McLean's alto and Bill Hardman's trumpet sound mesmerized us and connected us to what was happening in New York New York was our mecca too way back then because the music we loved was played there, and when we heard the music made in New York by New York musicians in those years, we were galvanized by all the worldly sophistication.

Listening to jazz music was serious to me and Rashid, and later on when we began using our homes as Black Community African Omnidevelopment Space Complexes, we would wonder out loud how we could have developed had we had some elder brothers in our neighborhood who would open up their homes for cultural and music centers. That is why each album me and Rashid had was so holy during one of our Golden musical moments in the 1950s.

During that time we got Curtis Fuller's album New Trombone, again on a Saturday in 1957, and we memorized that album by listening to it over and over again. We just kept it on the box and let it play over and over as we lay there listening. I know that album all they way in my grave beyond death and into eternity. New Trombone with Sonny "Red" Kyner, Hank Jones, Doug Watkins and Louis Hayes carried me completely away from many of my friends and their socializing fraternities.

I started chasing the music I loved, and the music I was chasing took me away from people who ended up in prison. The music I loved pushed me away from any distractions. This saved me from hanging out with the people that were my peers. They went to prison and I kept listening and listening.

In 1958, my father asked me and Rashid what we were going to do when we finished high school in June. We told him we wanted to join the Air Force. He fully agreed with our plan, but he asked us to hold off going until in the Fall of 1959. He wanted us to take a year off and just relax, rest, regroup, and do anything we wanted to do within structure and goodness, and then go into the Air Force fully refreshed, reinvigorated and revitalized.

The Summer of 1958 and the Summer of 1959 gave us the introduction to Lee Morgan on the album Moanin by Art Blakey Messengers of Benny Golson, Jymie Merrit, Bobby Timmons and on Horace Silver's with Blue Mitchell, Junior Cook, Gene Taylor and Louis Hayes. Soultrane by John Coltrane, Tenor Madness by Sonny Rollins, Brilliant Corners Thelonious Monk, Round About Midnight, Miles Davis, Milestones, Miles Davis, Silver Blue, Horace Silver, Sounds of Yusef, Yusef Lateef. This was our record collection up to 1960 and our 4 years in the Air Force. All these albums gave me and Rashid our identity, purpose and centeredness during 1955, 1956, 1957, 1958 and 1959.

If we would have not had those records at that historical period, we could easily be in a grave or broken mentally and spiritually. All the hours Rashid and I spent listening to the music we loved gave us our identity at such a young age that it carried over into our own imagery and image. We totally identified with the jazz musicians we idolized. Rashid loved Miles so much that he wanted a trumpet, and when he heard Lee Morgan in 1958, he asked my father to get him one. When my father got him a trumpet, he took his lessons weekly at Grinnell's, and everyday I would lay in my bed listening to him practice.

At that time, I had no real interest in any instrument — but that changed when I first heard the power of Paul Chambers' bass on Round About

Midnight, Miles Davis' first album on Columbia with Red Garland, Philly Joe Jones and John Coltrane. In fact, I grew to love Paul Chambers so very much that I named my first son, Paul Lawrence Dunbar Chambers.

    1958 was also the year that Rashid and I discovered the after hours jam sessions in Detroit at the West Inn that Yusef Lateef and his band hosted on Friday and Saturday nights after 2am. We spent a lot of Saturday mornings there listening and rubbing shoulders with all the musicians who came to play. We saw Roy Brooks, Frank Morelli, Terry Pollard, Ali Jackson, Harold and Ray McKinney, Frank Gant, Ernie Farrow and a lot of young dynamic musicians who totally amazed us with their musical artistry. The West Inn was the first time live music venue that we had ever been into — and I loved being around all those musical instruments. The bass violin fascinated me, and even though, I was dreaming about one day having one — at that time all I could do was stare at it in pure amazement. All week, Rashid and I lived to get back down to the West Inn to hang around all the hip musicians and be hypnotized by Roy Brooks' drums and Eric Farrow's bass.

AIR FORCE

1959-1963

On November 11, 1959, we entered the United States Air Force and we were shipped from Fort Wayne, Detroit to San Antonio, Texas. The Air Force basic training was a breeze and we did our basic training in just 5 weeks because Rashid and I were in an accelerated program that saw us shipped across base to the medical training school. It was here that we continued to add more jazz records to the record collection that we had locked up in our mother's closet at home.

In medical school, we went to school all day until 4:30pm, had base liberty until 10pm and every weekend we had passes to go to town. But, when Rashid and I went to the PX, we discovered that they had a jazz section, and it was there that we bought Cookin, Walkin, Relaxin and Dig by Miles Davis — and we would go over to our station's day room and listen to our music. We spent all of our off duty time in that very comfortable and warm spot — and we were able to introduce some of our friends to the music we loved.

    The Air Force gave us another music listening post, and when we left Texas in February 1960 for a 13 day leave, we brought our new Miles Davis albums to add to our collection. Of course, we went straight to Art's Record Store when we got home and brought quite a few albums on Blue Note, Prestige and Riverside. After our leave was up, we arrived at Hunter's Air Force Base in Savannah, Georgia, wide-eyed, excited and with all of our record albums. After we cleared the base and received our back pay, we went to the base PX and found that there was an excellent jazz record department that was loaded with many, many jazz records all for the discount price of $2.80 to 3.00. After we purchased a small T.V. and a small stereo for our room, we bought about 20 new albums. That is how we spent our first day in Savannah, in our room digging tunes and relishing our new music listening spot.

    Every pay day we spent almost half on attaining new albums and soon our record collection grew and grew. Our room became the hang out for all of our Air Force brothers, and on the weekend everybody would just stay in our room to be educated by us on the music we loved. We subscribed to Downbeat and Metronome magazines and discovered a Black record store that had all the Blue Note albums. I remember the first time that I went there on my first time going to Savannah, and I bought Horace Silver's new album Horacescope with Blue Mitchell, Junior Cook, Gene Taylor and Roy Brooks replacing Louis Hayes on drums. After I bought it I could not get back to the base fast enough. I listened to that album all night remembering all the many times I had seen Roy Brooks in Detroit at the West Inn.

The four years that Rashid and I spent in Savannah, Georgia at Hunter Air force Base was one of the greatest musical highlight times we could have. We educated our barracks and the 809th medical group to jazz music by constantly talking the music we loved, by living and breathing jazz musicians and jazz music. We not only dressed like jazz musicians, but we carried our jazz records with us every day. Every night that we went to sleep, we had a stack of records on our room stereo to go to sleep by and every morning we woke, we listened to an album before we began our daily shift at the base hospital.

We worked in several departments at the base hospital. Rashid ended up in the outpatient clinic, and I ended my Air Force career in surgery and central supply, where I had a radio tuned to the local radio station that played jazz regularly. In fact, I volunteered for the midnight session in central supply where I could read all night, and I listened to a popular jazz program on the radio that played all the great jazz tunes from midnight to four in the morning. I used to call in my requests, and in doing so, I became good friends with the DJ, Walter Cunningham. He acknowledged me and Rashid as having a large jazz collection and knowing jazz music history much more than he did. We invited him onto the base several times to listen to our records and talk. We had a library of Downbeats and Metronome magazines, and we knew what all the great musicians were doing, where they were performing and the new record releases coming out.

The base hospital had a huge medical library and a regular library that had all the latest magazines, Time, Newsweek, Post, Life, Colliers, Esquire, Look, Readers Digest, New Yorker, Ebony, Vogue. Sports, the local newspaper the Savannah News, and I began reading the New York Times in that library during my time on the midnight shift. I worked from 11-7, but every night I had my job done, and I read and wrote letters and studied most of the time. One cup of coffee was like a 5 hour energy supply, and I never fell asleep because I was so wired up. Rashid and I bought an electric coffee maker, and we drank hot chocolate and Maxwell's Coffee with the brothers who came to our room to listen to music.

You could smell the coffee brewing in the hallways near our barrack room and hear the jazz out of our room incessantly. Rashid and I were known for our love of jazz music and for our huge record collection that was dedicated to our love of jazz. We did not run around in Savannah drinking, getting drunk and chasing women. We drank our coffee, and on occasion, cold beer, and we chased after the jazz records that we saw advertised in Downbeat and Metronome. One of our friends, Ronald Gibbs, played baritone, and we would go to the Savannah bowling alley sometimes to hear him play in the Saturday night jam sessions that local musicians held. One night the bass player let me play on his bass, and that was my first experience of trying to play it. That experience stuck to me like glue and made me really want a bass violin in 1961, but it did not sink in at the time that I would ever own one.

In 1962, Rashid and I really loved Miles Davis' band with Paul Chambers, Red Garland, Philly Joe Jones and Hank Mobley (after Trane had left); Art Blakey's band with Freddie Hubbard, Curtis Fuller, Wayne Shorter, Cedar Walton and Reggie Workman and the classic John Coltrane Quartet with McCoy Tyner, Jimmy Garrison, and Elvin Jones plus Eric Dolphy, and we would speculate on how we would love seeing them. So, once we followed them in Downbeat, we knew where they were performing all the time.

When we found out Coltrane would be at the Minor Key in Detroit, I took a 6 day leave and went all way to Pontiac to go see that band. I never forgot that trip. I left Savannah that Wednesday morning in the early winter month of 1962 and arrived in Detroit about 8pm Thursday night. I spent Friday hanging out with my family and friends, and that Saturday night I was one of the first people at the Minor Key, sitting right there close to the stage when Trane, Eric Dolphy, McCoy, Jimmy Garrison and Elvin hit. They played until 4 in the morning and it was one of the greatest nights in my life.

    Trane played so long and hard that I was completely overwhelmed by the sheer power of his solos. He took a long opening solo, and his second solo taking the song out was so long that I could not believe how spiritually strong he was — he seemed totally possessed; and Jimmy Garrison seemed like he was a machine the way he pushed, grimaced and locked into the bass. Eric Dolphy played so viciously and long that I thought he would never end his solos. McCoy Tyner was unbelievable too, and he played long and beautifully crafted piano solos. Then there was Elvin: he played so hard that puddles of water appeared under the drums from all the sweat pouring out of him. After the music ended, I talked to him, telling him that I had been to his family home many times in my relationship with his niece, her mother and his sisters. When he hugged me, he was soaking wet and he could wring out the suit he had on.

When I got home to Pontiac that morning — I did not even go to bed — I caught the Greyhound bus back to Savannah to tell Rashid and the fellows of my time with Trane that Monday night. Rashid did the same thing when he caught the Art Blakey Jazz Messengers at the Minor Key when he was home on a short leave. We never did catch the Horace Silver Quintet or Miles Davis during that time, but we had their albums, and their early 1960 albums fed our musical imagination every time we listened to them. When we honorably discharged from the Air Force on November 11, 1963, we brought home a huge record collection and an even bigger love for jazz.

When Rashid and I went into the Air Force in 1959, we were beyond color — we were into human beingness, and that was a unique strength of mind to have in a world of diversity. We sailed right through 4 years of the military world almost 1,000 miles away in a southern town in deep Georgia. From February 15, 1960 to November 11, 1963, we had the most ardent support, loyal protection and above all, the most illuminating love we could ever hope to receive from everyone who touched out lives with purpose.

Rashid and I were given a freedom of expression that only we could have expressed culturally, intellectually and spiritually. Rashid and I were unique in our synergistic bond with everyone who smiled with their teeth and hearts. We were able to create our uniqueness for 4 years on Hunter Air Force base. We decorated our room like it was a listening library, and there were pictures of Miles, Trane, Mingus, Sonny Rollins and modern abstract art filling up the walls.I still have pictures of that room's spiritual power. I listened to hours and hours of music in that shrine of peaceful harmony.

I loved that room — you know, I slept in the music like I slept in a dream. I schooled my whole 804th medical group from that room with my being beyond color uniqueness. I rubbed shoulders with doctors, colonels, captains, 30 year sergeants who'd fought in World War II and Korea. I worked every day with people beyond color and I always had white brothers with whom I lived and breathed family. I lived a charmed life, the ideal life for me during my beautiful Air Force career.

I made my transitional move back to my parents' home when I left a party at the 804th medical group Thursday, November 7th, 1963 with Rashid in self fulfilled gratitude for all the love everyone gave with total abandonment. On November 8, 1963 we received an honorable discharge and left Hunter Air Force Base not looking back on 4 years of history and memory but looking casually at the future.

We had no plans, or no thoughts, about what we were going to do. We led a charmed life, a life so resilient and tenacious as the music we love. We put our fate into the music we loved, lived, breathed — and were fastly becoming. Rashid and I stayed in Savannah with friends Friday and Saturday — and that Sunday November 11, 1963 at high noon, we caught a smoking Greyhound bus that saw us arrive at the Detroit Greyhound bus station around 8pm.

CULTURE WAR

New Music by the AfricanOmniDevelopmentSpace Complex

بسم الله الرحمن الرحيم
In the Name of Allah, The Beneficent, The Merciful

WE NE

PONTIAC

1963-1972

We came back to our first scene of music in our hometown of birth loaded inside and out with the music we had listened to in the Air Force music center and we had a legendary record collection that defined our musical focal and cultural thinking. We moved right back into our room, and my parents loved us for being home with our music. My parents were open-minded, and they cherished the time we were at home, But, Rashid and I got jobs a week after we got home.

That Monday, November 18, 1963, he was working at Shaw's jewelry in Downtown Pontiac and I hired in for my first day of a 30 year (1963-1993) lesson-of-life-school working at General Motors, Pontiac Motors Division. I flashed my D.D. form 214 showing my Air Force honorable discharge and I had a life long job that 30 years until this has sustained me in my love of life, spirituality, and supported all my loves that give reasons for living. Again, Pontiac

Motors instantly became part of my family structure. I received absolutely no mixed messages. I was given the wings of encouragement, inspiration, and the opportunity to evolve and develop into my aspirations and dreams.

Working at Pontiac Motors was a big adjustment, but what I loved about working so steadily was the weekly check that let me buy the music every week at KD's record store. 1963, 1964, 1965, 1966, 1967 were wonderful years because I moved into my own spot, 225 South Marshall, Pontiac, Michigan, and I turned it into a Black music and Black art cultural center with my huge record collection as the foundation of my cultural spirituality.

At that time Rashid and I began going to the Drome Showbar Lounge on Glendale and Dexter, a West Side area that we knew well from our summers spent in Detroit with relatives. We saw a lot of the bands we used to dream about seeing when we read the Downbeats and the Drome became our home. We saw Horace Silver, Joe Henderson, Trane with Pharoah Sanders, Jimmy Garrison, Alice Coltrane, Rashid Ali, McCoy Tyner, Freddie Waits, Herbie Lewis, Art Blakey, Bill Hardman, Woody Shaw, Tyrone Washington, Larry Ridley, Roger Humphries, Freddie Hubbard, James Spaulding, Mike Lawrence, Billy Harper, The Jazz Crusaders, Slide Hampton, Junie Booth, Hugh Walker, Pepper Adams, Yusef Lateef, Cecil McBee, James

Black, Reggie Workman, Mike Nock, George Arvantis, Roy Brooks, Hugh Lawson. Grachan Moncur III, Bobby Hutchinson, and each one of the musicians deeply, profoundly and inspiringly influenced and impacted my life.

It was also at this time that we started following Melvin "Bubby" Hatchett, Pontiac's renowned and legendary pianist, home from doing time at Jackson Prison due to his heroin drug habit. Bubby had learned from the famous Hank Jones from his residence right across the street from the Jones' family home. He was a master musician who was in charge of Washington Junior and Pontiac High School, and he could play any instrument. The trio he had in Jackson Prison was taught by him, and Jesse the bass player and Slim the drummer with Bubby on piano was one of my favorite bands. We followed then down to their Friday and Saturday gig at the Spot Bar on 12th street and back out to Pontiac for their after hours gig at LaRoach's Tea and their Sunday matinee gig at 4:30 pm. Bubby brought some Detroit musicians to play with him at La Roach and I was exposed to Joe Thurman, George Bohanan and some hard swinging tenor saxophonists that I can not recall their names.

Jessie the bass player started encouraging me to play the bass when he found out that I loved the bass violin. He was the first one in 1967 that gave me my vision of actually having a bass and playing one.

However, it was Rashid attaining his trombone around that time; and one of our long time mentors, Ahmed Jihad Malik Shabazz, who finally convinced me to seriously pursue my bass love dream when he opened up his Ahmed African Import Shop up on North Saginaw next to KD record store in the spring of 1968. Ahmed and Rashid started getting together at the back of the African Import Shop to play and they pushed me very hard until I went out and attained my bass in the fall of 1968. I got the bass, and Rashid and Ahmed and I came up with the name.The Fireworks Art Ensemble came together every Friday, Saturday and Sunday to hit as hard as we could — based on sound, strength, feelings and lengths of time as our musical philosophy at that time.

Ahmed African Import Shop in 1968 became our journey of playing music every Friday night wherever the spirit took us. Ahmed, Rashid and I created a music and art music space in the back of the shop, made a stage, chipped in and purchased a piano. I just jumped on our bandstand with my bass every Friday night and taking Saturday lessons.

There is a lot of work in me that's been contributed by a lot of people. When I began playing the bass violin, I had tremendous support from every corner of my life. Letting them know about having my dream up front and personal every time I came home from work was my proudest moment. I wore my bass love like a badge of honor — it became my centeredness.

I lived for Friday nights, and from 1968 to 1971, we played with a rich array of all kinds of musicians, local, from Detroit and international. Besides the piano, we had African drums, djembe, congo, all kinds of percussion, bells, even had a gong, claves, tambourines, C melody saxophone, and a big box full of handmade percussion instruments. Many, many Friday nights we filled the air with a raucous unrelenting roar that could not roar high enough or long enough.

We spent many Friday nights blasting away until the sun came up. Afterwards we would go over to Nick's Place in downtown Pontiac for a big breakfast and go home and sleep until we woke up tired.

We used to play at a small club on Pontiac's west side called Teddy's on Monday nights and with Ahmed on drums, me on bass, Rashid on trombone, Hubert price on alto. We used to stretch all the way out from 10 until 2am. Sometimes we played concerts at the shop on Saturday and Sunday afternoon. We played a lot at the Pontiac Black Cultural Center with poets and speakers. We played on street corners, in the projects, Boys Clubs, other people's basements, Oakland University, Wayne State, my apartment, Ahmed's basement, a bean soup restaurant, playgrounds. We played at a McGovern political rally, Hayes Jones' youth center several times.

One of the most memorable times happened in 1969. Ahmed and I ventured down to Baker's Keyboard Lounge to catch the Art Blakey Jazz Messengers with Donald Smith, piano, Ramon Morris, tenor, Bill Hardman, trumpet and a Japanese bass player. We hooked up with them, and after the last set was over, we had made arrangements to pick them up the next morning and bring them out to dinner in Pontiac the next day. Art Blakey and Bill Hardman could not make it, but Donald Smith, Ramon Morris and the Japanese bass player joined us out in Pontiac for a banquet feast, some powerful reefer, and an ambience of good food, good boo and unbridled love and admiration for their devotion to the music they traveled all over the world playing. Afterwards we went back up to the shop and played music until they had to get back to Detroit to play the night's gig. Donald Smith came back to Pontiac many times, and I had an opportunity to play in a trio setting with him in Ahmed's basement all night long, I closed my eyes when we first began playing, and when I opened my eyes we had played a beautiful length of time.

So — Length of Time became my musical mantra. I found out that the longer you played, the stronger you became musically and spiritually. The longer you played, the stronger and passionate the music came driven by the spiritual energy of playing longer, louder, higher with all the strength of spirit you could muster. Praising in the spirit of the music and dancing in the spirit of the music. The bass violin is an instrument that takes tremendous strength and in order to command any mastery on it — you have to play it thousands and thousands of X times X. My spirit was the only source I had to be a bass workhorse and mule on the bass. I had absolutely no training — I just played and played and sweated and sweated and that is how I developed.

Also — in 1969 — I began going down to Abdul Samad's attic loft to play with him on drums, and the legendary Charles Miles on tenor, alto, flute and soprano and African drums. I played with them many all day Saturdays and Sundays. Then I also played with Faruq Z Bay - tenor, Jalil Bey - alto, voice, Charles Solomon - oud. Saadi - trombone, congas, Hakim - tenor, Abdul Rahman - drums, a local Detroit repertory troupe, dancers and a host of percussion players. This band played all over Detroit and in Windsor, Canada, at Wayne State and Northwest Community Center.

Two of the most legendary times that I had playing bass violin with the First Primal Rhythm Arkestra occurred when we supplied the music during a year residency at the Concert East theater on the east side of Adams and Woodward every Friday and Saturday night backing a host of revolutionary Black actors, actresses and dancers. We assembled an almost 20 piece band based on letting anyone who possessed an instrument to join up in the cacophony of our music, supporting and inspiring those in the cast of The Black Ark, a play written by LeRoi Jones (Amiri Baraka).

After that event was over, we would go over to the Ferry Street Coffee House on Ferry and John R. and play alternating sets with David Durrah, John Dana, Danny Spencer. But some occasions we would have the Ferry Street Coffee House all to ourselves and we would scream at the top of our spirit to drown you out and we would really go "OUT."

Out music became our calling card and became well known enough to be invited to the University of Windsor as an "out music band" under a new creation named The Bey Family. The school sent a van to pick us up, gave us the money to rent a station wagon, and we arrived at a full fledged festival on this Friday in October 1969. About 30 had made the trip across the river, and we were feted like music royalty playing music out of the tradition of Sun Ra, The Chicago Art Ensemble, Archie Shepp, the Chicago A.A.C.M.. Most of us had come into music without any at all musical training, basics, fundamentals, techniques.

We were all ear playing, blowing away, flailing, trying to take our music "OUT" in the only place we knew. In fact, I never even attempted to tune my bass, I had absolutely no tonal pitch because I was completely tone deaf. Like Shelley Manne said, "We never played the same song once." We never attempted to play any song — we just played as hard as we could, as long and as loud as we could and let the spirit take over. Someone always stepped to the podium with the spirit that carried the music and who excited and inspired the band.

That night at the University of Windsor, we hit the stage in full regalia of our "OUT" music reputation, and for 3 hours we raged, postured, screamed bloody murder, died on the cross, arose from the dead and became completely reborn to live on. It is a beautiful sight to see 30 people all so possessed and locked into a spiritual trance praise dance with dancers leaping, whirling and dancing to about 10 pulsating African drummers, percussionists, flute, and, and grand piano, bass violin and drums.

After we played we were ushered into a small banquet hall and served a massive feast of food, tons of fruit and vegetable trays, mountains of hors d'oeurves, sandwiches, and I was introduced that night to Molson Ale.

Around that time I got my first two Sun Ra albums by sending to ESP records for The Heliocentric Worlds of Sun Ra volumes I and II and Bells by Albert

Ayler. Also, I had fallen in love with Archie Shepp and his musical philosophy of playing music not based on chords, keys, scales, music theory, technique, knowledge, but simply to play music based on sound strength and energy. Play exclusively what it is you feel in the moment, something never even conceived, something raw, guttural and utterly spiritual. Call "OUT" the spirit from the spirit in the spirit and ride the spirit to play the music as hard and as long as you are in the spirit.

My record library developed with the music that I listened to in the late 1960s, and I loved Trane's direction that brought me to Archie Shepp, John Gilmore, Ronnie Boykins, Albert Ayler. The Impulse record albums that I was assembling and the music that I was playing gave me great incentive into 1970, 1971, 1972, 1973 and 1974. The music that I was listening to influenced and impacted me every step that I took. My record library blossomed and bloomed and groomed all the early 1970s.

I was living at 225 South Marshall, upstairs over my sister's family when I met patrick brennan down at the Ibo Cultural Center one Sunday Matinee digging one of my favorite McCoy Tyner quartets with Calvin Hill on bass and I think Sonny Fortune on alto — and could it have been Alphonse Mouzon on drums? The Ibo Cultural Center was a university for me in the school of New York musicians, and I attended class there regularly on Saturday nights and Sunday matinees. I took notes, mentally, spiritually and I wanted to know whether they were vegetarians. To me, the New York musicians are international world artists, masters of the music that burns into my deepest love, my deepest identification and my most ardent support.

Rashid, Ahmed and I met a lot of great musicians at the Ibo Cultural Center. It was there one Saturday in another band that was absolutely my favorite McCoy quartet band with Byard Lancaster on alto, I think Calvin Hill or Herbie Lewis on bass and on drums was a legendary drummer from the Philadelphia music scene. I love Byard Lancaster to this day. He blew so hard and furiously, and so long and so high, that I didn't want him to stop. He blew every mind that I had possessed and created a new hearing the fire power of the alto saxophone, and I carry the experience of Byard Lancaster with me in my history and memory.

I took what Byard Lancaster gave me and tried to play my bass as hard and as fierce and as long and as high as I could for as long as I could. That became my bass style, the longer the stronger — then let the spirit take charge and ride the spirit. Byard Lancaster was one of my music professors and I loved learning at the feet of his fire music making. A glowing red hot fire music maker and I took the lessons that I learned from my many New York master musicians that the University of the Ibo Cultural Center brought in for master classes in the music I loved.

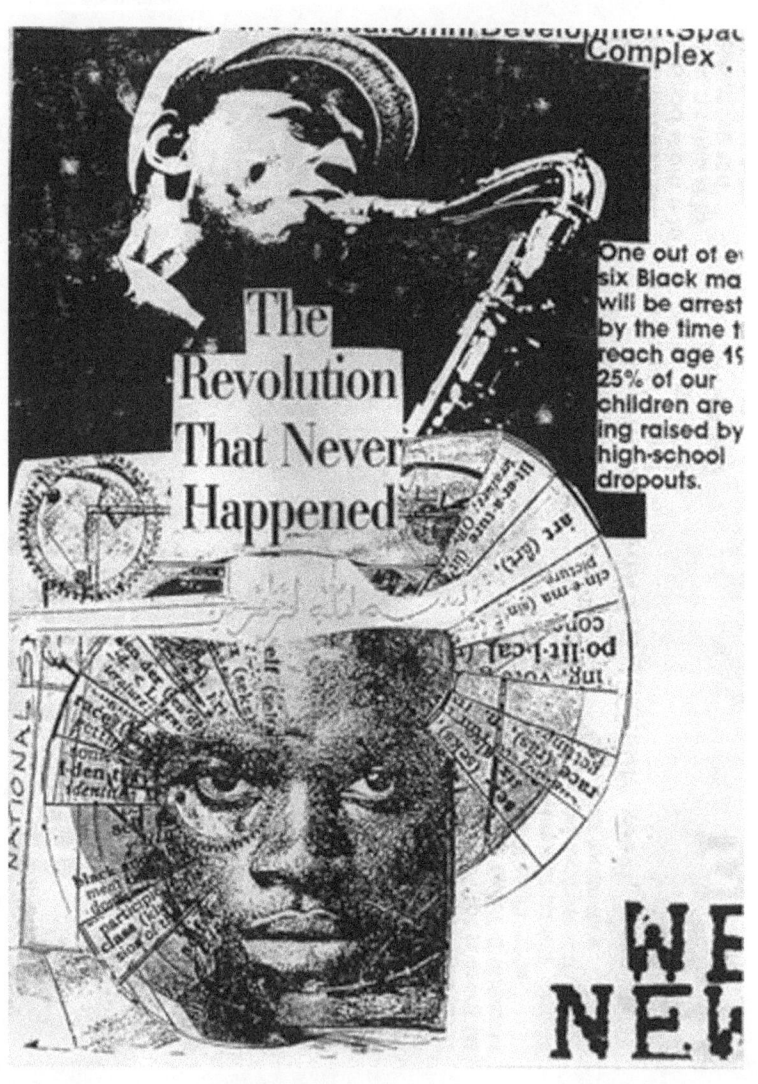

The African Omni-development Space Complex / We New

The power of the minds we had inherited directly from destiny outrunning fate. Our history continues to speak for itself. Every musical experience that I had in my lifelong love for music made me the music that I always played.

I composed my own music from all the music that was put into me form birth. I am all the music I heard, just like I am all the food that I shit, all the water I have drunk to piss out, I am all the music I have laid in, loved in, pained and suffered in and all the music I lived. I was not just playing and listening to music. I was living the music every day.

I got away with it by not fronting — but taking my music with me — even to all of Pontiac Motors. For years I had been writing poetry, and I carried a book bag full of books, dictionaries, paper, pens, and every chance I got I was reading and writing. Everybody loved and supported my sincerity and watched me become an African proud elder, African scholar and African genius. All Rashid and I did was to keep on letting our music lead and let our visions and dreams come to us.

1972 was the year that I met Michael Carey and Tyrone Bilbo through Michael Reed, and a young brother who had joined me, Ahmed and Rashid on Fridays at the African Import Shop. At that time I had a trombone, clarinet, alto horn, baritone horn, alto recorders, a trumpet and some percussion instruments that I had made. We began having formal sessions at my apartment collectively on Thursdays — and it became a cultural center every day of the week.

Rashid became the agent of our music gigs, and during that period of 1972 we played at Oakland University, St. George's Church, the Holiday Inn, the Sheraton Inn, basements, Boys and Girls Clubs, and we played up on the corner of Bagley and Wesson, a block from the home of Elvin Jones at a bean soup cafe.

The rich history of 1972 brought beautiful closeness to all of us, Michael Carey began playing piccolo, flute, bass clarinet, tenor and alto. Tyrone Bilbo played baritone, Michael Reed played alto, Rashid played trombone, trumpet and Ahmed played drums. On our regular Thursday music sessions at my apartment, I would cook and we would sit down to eat and talk. And out of these talks came our 1972 music to ride to the future: The African Omni-development Space Complex.

In May of 1973, I moved to 92 N. Ardmore one Saturday morning, and the first thing that I brought within these walls was my bass violin. I wanted a home to play my music in — and I was not going to play in the basement. I wanted music to be home and music to be on all the time. I wanted to play every day — and that is what I did. I played music with everybody who came through my door. I bought a set of drums, a piano and I played all the music I loved playing.

I never really thought of having a home concert series or cooking meals for people who came to support the music. However, I was deeply into vitamins, the health food store, wheat germ oil, herb teas, yogurt, organic foods, the Oakland County Farmers' Market, honey, fresh vegetables, fruits. I had bought a juicer and I drank quarts of carrot juice, orange juice and apple juice, and I also drank a bottle of Korean ginseng every week. As a Sunni Orthodax Muslim, I was praying 5 times a day and I put everything that I was doing physically, culturally and spiritually into the music I was playing.

From January 1, 1974, I began keeping a meticulous and detailed written journal through January 1, 1975 of all the times that I played my bass with anyone and everyone who came through my door

— and I mean I played with people walking past my house as much as I did people coming to my house to play. I had a house full of instruments, and I recruited the world of Pontiac, Detroit, New York, the projects, the dope house, Jackson Prison and the graveyard. I played with people from all over the world, if I saw a spark in your eye, I would become a taskmaster and give you an instrument to play every day. I played with a shifting band of new members. I had a young boys and girls band. I played bass with everybody.

Among the entries in my journal, On Saturday, December 21, 1974, Abdul Jalil Bey played alto, percussion with Faruq Z. Bey on alto, Abdul Rauf piano, Abdul Khafils - bass violin, Abdul Samrod (Skeeter Shelton) - tenor, Fareed McKnight - tenor, flute, patrick brennan - alto, bass viol, Kawi - clarinet, Yusef - tenor, clarinet, Sadiq - drums. Abdul Halim - drums, Michael Carey - bass, clarinet, piccolo, Jomo - trumpet, Abdul Rahman - bass violin and I played bass violin, trombone. We played 1.) Ode For 2.) Song Africa 3.) Expanding 4.) Song. Love 5.) Coming out into Out 6.) Suchness 7.) Copped Bopped 8.) Longer is Shorter 9.) Future 10.) The Ceremony Wedding

I was soaking up and absorbing history and memory supported by my huge faith in music in action. 1975 was a gallant quest from January to December. I played music all during the week with anyone coming through my door, and on the weekends I celebrated playing my bass violin with the musicians who were nurtured and empowered in the music we loved playing. Week after week, weekend after weekend, the music was kept at a "heightened existence." The fires of Black unstoppable anger and Black unstoppable love never ceased.

I have played my bass violin all the way to 2002 from those 1975 years at my home music and art center. I have kept extensive written documented journals that I find a great delight and historically a coup. I play my bass violin many times, and when I go through the pages of my history and memory, I can read and remember point blank the musicians who came to my house, the powerful music played.

I can remember all the ardent support, loyal protection and above all, the love from my N. Ardmore, Michigan Street, N. Francis street neighbors, my Sanford Arms apartment neighbors, my N. Sanford Street neighbors, my Lois Street neighbors who never called the police on me and protected as mightily as they did.

They would tell me "that they would hear the drums" — and they would sit outside in summer and listen to the music pouring out of my house at 3 in the morning with complete abandon. Today, all the children who lived on N. Ardmore remember, reflect and reminisce about how much they loved Friday nights when they hung outside late listening to a Black hot music that played and played and did not stop even in their most distant and near dreams.

I was watched over and protected all those years that I played cutting edge music at my African Space Complex home. I tried to make the people who came to play better with the music and take it as far as they possibly could with even harder work, high aspirations and ambition.

Rashid and I did not have older brothers in the community who shared their homes as cultural and music centers, educational centers and Black think tanks and African Space Complexes. Everyone who knew me understood exactly what I was doing and all I had was everyone's love.

Whenever you came to my house in 1975 and saw a white face, it was a white brother that came to my house like I also came to his house and a white brother who was in my Pontiac Motors family. I had so many great friends who gave me chunks of their complete friendship. There is John Karazian, an Armenian alto player from the early bebop era who worked with me, and he loved music. When he found out I was serious about playing the bass violin, he tutored me for months, brought his alto to my house and played lots of sets with us. He became a Friday night regular inspiring me at work and at home.

Howard McGray came to all of the gigs that we did on Monday nights at O.J.'s and he and Tiger Pearson made a big collage out of the flyers that I made. They put it up on the wall at Charley' Jazz Bar and Grille in Pontiac. Porter Williamson and I worked side by side at Pontiac Motors and he got me paying gigs at his church's men's programs and at dinners at the Sheraton Inn. I had a white brother, George O'Shea, who gave me a trombone. He brought it to work to see if I could play it, and I played a ten minute ramble, shamble and shuffle.

Everybody at Pontiac Motors had their own thing going on. I networked with everyone because I was raised beyond color having mystically and spiritually connected with my white brothers. I love good people and good people love me. I can testify and tout the testament of all the people who shared their human goodness with me and touched my life with the goodness of their purpose.

I had a beautiful friend, Carl Lightfoot, whom I worked with, who was a student at University of Michigan. He drove to Ann Arbor on school days and also attended Oakland Community College. He came to many of our musical sets, shot a lot of very memorable pictures. Carl Lightfoot quit Pontiac Motors when he attained a scholarship to Columbia University in 1978. I treasured his intellectual input that he brought to me and I know that he is very successful and a giant of his vision. He taught the value of an education and hard work to all of us who were listening to him watching and photographing us.

Because Rashid and I received so much support and love, you could never tell who would be coming through. In the course of time I put a sign-in book by my telephone, and today I can look through the pages of time and see all the the hundreds of names of visitors to the African Space Complex. The bass violin has allowed me to serenade pages of people from all walks of their lives who have walked into my music. They walked their talk into my presence of music.

Among the musicians who came to my home on a regular basis in the 1972-1975 era, let me introduce Kalunji – alto, soprano whom I met when he was 16. Rashid and I recruited him as the first member of the African Space Complex. At the time, he was the president of the Pontiac Northern Association for Black Students and editor of the school paper. When we met him, he was overwhelmed by the music and joined forces with us immediately by acquiring a clarinet and soon was playing alto and soprano saxophone with raw fire. He quickly became our main voice of creative dissonance and fine spirit.

When Kalunji brought them to me, Michael Carey was playing piccolo, flute, bass clarinet and alto clarinet and Tyrone Bilbo, the son of a preacher, was a baritone player and a musical charmer full of musical delights and with an urgency that would not quit. The kindred spirits that I was surrounded by were contributing unapologetically and unashamedly to the music we lived and died in. Believe me, a lot of brothers died horrible deaths as well as lived lives of success and wellness — but that story is much too long to tell. Let me give you some names of the other people who were playing in my home with us and deserve to be mentioned in history and memory.

Yusef Abdul Rahim was 14. He was the youngest nephew of Thad, Hank and Elvin Jones and the most talented of all the Jones' next generation. He played first chair clarinet in the Pontiac Central Band, played tenor and soprano with his own musical groups, played with me constantly and studied under a renowned symphonic music teacher.

Thomas Peter Jones was a prodigy, another Pontiac legend and another nephew of Thad, Hank and Elvin who became Pontiac's number one drummer after Elvin. Peter Jones had a legendary childhood in the same home that Elvin Jones was raised in and was the baby in the house with his crib in the same room Elvin practiced in. He became a childhood star on the drums practicing for hours. He became so strong on the drums that he was called "The Blacksmith." But, he could not overcome his addiction to heroin and consequently, whenever he was out of prison for a short time, we would get bits and pieces of drum mastery amid the fire of Elvin Jones in his drumming marathons. He loved to play everyone down into the floor and then hammer, hammer and hammer and hammer at the drums. I loved to play with him because I truly had to be a mule workhorse to be heard by him. I had to make him play with me and then against me. He and I played all by ourselves a lot. I had to build up my stamina, arms, wrists, hands, fingers, shoulders and back to play against being against with him. It was like playing against a hurricane.

The legendary drummer Abdul Samad had a loft on Vancouver, and everybody in Detroit knew that he played 7 days a week with anyone who came to play. Abdul Samad and I hooked up a spiritual unity thing the very first time we played together at his loft in 1971. He made playing music so smooth. It was with him that I started closing my eyes when the music started, and when I opened up my eyes the set was all over. Ahmed Samad and I could play note for note with each other because we thought in the same musical patterns and codes. He and I talked on drums and bass as though we were talking to our ancestors of Ancient Egypt and Ancient Antiquity. I also spent a lot of time playing with just him, and he was a teacher of all kinds of ancient new music.

I met Detroit's underground musical wizard and legend Charles Miles at Abdul Samad's loft. Charles

Miles played like Byard – alto – Lancaster with a fiery, screaming and all consuming urgency. He never let up on his intensity and played on and on and on and on. He played tenor, alto, piccolo and flute.

I was fortunate to have had the opportunities to play some wonderful and amazing long hours with only Abdul Samad and Charles. That valuable experience gave me the power to come back to Pontiac and share the music lessons that I received from two of Detroit's most legendary musicians.

Abdul Halim came from both Peter Jones and Abdul Samad. They took time with him at age 14, and he took time with them to learn to love the drums as much as they did. He and I played together every chance we got and we loved playing against each other.

Just as significant was Umam Saladim – flute. piccolo, bass clarinet, tenor and alto. He also was a nephew of Thad, Hank and Elvin Jones. He too had been raised in his grandmother Olivia Jones' household and played music as natural and effortlessly as he breathed. He also was first chair woodwinds in Pontiac Central Symphonic Band, took private lessons from a symphonic classic teacher, spent a summer at Interlochen Music Camp. When he went into the army in 1972, he played in the 8th Army Band stationed in Germany.

Pete Washington was here with me during my early 1970s. He played alto and he loved Bird, knew all of Bird's music and played it for all of us to become familiar with the music of bebop. Pete Washington was totally invaluable. He loved to laugh — and whenever he played a musical phrase that he loved — he would laugh out loud and really get involved in his horn.

Our pianist Hakim was also a first chair musician out of the Pontiac Central Band. He had a basement music studio at his parents' home and we all loved playing there. In fact, we would play at his house in early afternoon and come over to my house to play deep into the night. Other times we started playing at my house and later went to Hakim's studio for the night and early morning.

Faruq Z. Bey loved coming to Pontiac to play in the atmosphere of my African Space Complex and cultural music Black center. The Black wall that I had painted 2 coated layers deep created a creative offering that I loved playing music into the "blood in my eye." Faruq Z. Bey and I evolved musically together from our days of playing together with First Primal Rhythm Arkestra, and we stayed connected. He made his musical genius felt musically and brought the most musical spirituality out of my bass violin playing.

I have always been indebted to how seriously he took being a musician. It was "as serious as life" to him and he would lock his doors and lock out the world for weeks playing his horns and practicing a discipline that rewarded him with his magical musical genius. He learned to read music, write music for all parts of a piece, orchestrate. He composed and transposed, notated, played tenor, soprano, Bb clarinet, bass clarinet, alto clarinet, piccolo, flute, congas, djembe, recorders and piano. He became a master musician, and he always came out to my house to play music with the Pontiac musician heirs and custodians of the Thad, Hank and Elvin Jones history and memory.

For example, Abdul Jalil Bey, who played alto, paid homage to the traditions of Thad, Hank and Elvin Jones in the early 1970s by coming to Pontiac weekly, and during some weekends with carloads of Detroit musicians who played at my house, in the streets and in other Pontiac homes, they brought dancers, percussionists. They sold African jewelry, incense, African clothes, books, African oils and African hats. They brought on all day African festivals and we played music loud and long to celebrate the good feelings of being Africans. Abdul Jalil Bey recognized in me a light of insightfulness, and he inspired me to keep playing my bass violin until my bass violin played me.

Abdul Jalil Bey loved playing at Mae Sams's after hours joint where all the hard core alcoholics and drunks came after all the stores, clubs and bars closed. On Friday and Saturday morning at 3 or 4 am, I would take my bass, and Abdul Jalil Bey would carry his alto to play with Blind George on piano. He too was a legend, and Mae Sam's had been his gig for decades. Blind George loved me and Abdul Jalil Bey. He came to my house many times, and the more musicians that played, the more robustly he played. He had a very acute ear and tuned everybody up to suit his ear. When we played at Mae Sam's — even though the audience would be nearly dead drunk — the music gave them life and they urged us to play hard and with passion. Blind George played every style — boogie woogie, blues, rock and roll, rhythm and blues, jazz and at any given time he could stretch all the way out "out."

Another fascinating musician that played with us was Jamal, who played trumpet. He joined us when he was 15, and he had never really known much about jazz trumpet. I hurried up and presented to him an album by Lee Morgan and he hurried up and became a Lee Morgan cult follower. Subsequently, I could name so many others that joined the African Omni-development Space Complex / We New. I have played with people who went to many corners of the world from my home.

Melvin Price became Pontiac's first Black musician to move to Switzerland in the late 1960s. He was also a first chair trombone player at Thomas

Jefferson and at Pontiac Central High, who along with his brother Donald Price, held jam sessions at his basement studio in his mother's south side home, and a lot of musicians were formed there. After he got out of high school, he played his trombone and congas all over Detroit and Pontiac. He worked briefly at GM, and the next message I received from him, he was in Europe, living, playing his trombone and congas and playing his music.

In fact, Melvin Price made two very timeless memorable albums that he gave me when he came home to visit family, friends and musicians. He usually came home every summer — and I knew when he walked into my house with his trombone that I was going to be treated to the person of a world traveling trombonist on fire and a force of music that had to be urgently supported. Melvin Price flew long, deep and ever deeper into an intensity that could have blown my walls and my walls still speak to me of his spirit.

Melvin Price could call out the spirit, but so could Joel Letvin, a Jewish clarinet player, a graduate of U of M, a Peace Corps member who had spent two years with the Wolof people in Senegal — and he loved jazz and African music. He had located recently to Pontiac to work, raise honeybees and to raise a family. We met at the Oakland County Farmers' Market and became fast friends in our Saturday talks, and soon he brought his clarinet to our Friday night sets. Joel

Letvin was with the African Omnidevelopment Space Complex on Fridays that saw the music levitate up out of the room to rock the world. He has never forgotten music where he could feel Africa in the same musical dance rhythm that he heard from morning to noon and deep into the night. That musical pushing the spirit and calling out the spirit to bring more spirit to trance dance into a higher spirit going higher to never come down.

Every couple years Joel Letvin will come to my door with jars of honey and with the fondest memories of a music where he rejoiced, sang his of his ancestors and celebrated himself.

All music is about celebration and I have had a life of music and celebration that was "unstoppable love." Studying 1975 again lets me really look at all the people who came to my home to play music that was not played anywhere in the world. We did not only play free music — we just played. Never did anyone at the African Space call out a standard tune or make mention of anyone's playing anybody's music but the music we played.

I am proud to say "We just played," and as I look at the year 1976, I look at all the names of the banner of Blackness that were played under whenever we played. Our music banners spoke for our consciousness, our spirituality, our commitment, our self determination, our resolve, our rescue, our restoration, our redemption and our rendezvous with a great destiny that awaits.

Here is a list of our music banner names in the great and grinding comeuppance. In other words — our cause of African Centeredness in being Black was glorified in the music. The Black Ark / The Black Planet / Cosmic Ceremony / The Black Fire Now / The Black Ark Speaks, African Space Cosmic Program / The Spawnin Ground / Song Light Complex / The Charcoal Sky / Forecast / Dhiker / Deeds / Focus De East / Nigh Vistant / Perfected Silence / Joined Forces.

As I turn the pages of my 1976 journal I can still feel the strength that I'd gained playing my bass for so many years in the comfort of my own home and having so many, many people come to play with me. For 30 years I was empowered to play all the goodness, all the Black Unstoppable Love that filled my musical soul.

I have a musical soul that's run over gallon glasses, that's run over rivers and oceans. I was born hearing the the pain and suffering of the slave ship, of the brutal horror and dehumanization of slavery. I was born in the blues storming through every Blackman and Blackwoman I've ever met in my life. Africa was my introduction into the music and 1976 is made real by the raging fire music I played.

I was supported by the members of Forecast all year long — Abdul Halim - druns, Abdul Mansa Hajj - violin, trumpet and flute and Fareed McKnight - tenor. I was able to recruit Musa Green, another Pontiac Central Band member, who was a wizard on tenor, alto and soprano. Also, a new drummer, Habib, joined us. He played in a funk band with a heavy interplay with the bass guitar. He and I had a ball. I loved to lock in with him and then take him places musically where only the spirit can go. He played with an expression of surprise, never knowing what I was going to play.

Malachi, who had been hanging out with us, bought himself a tenor and alto and came on board with us playing a furious band of fire music. He played each set like his world was on fire, so we called him "The Fireman."

My Pontiac Motors Family

There is a human warmth underneath the incessant buzz of life, and when I went into Pontiac Motors at age 23, I had to make it a learning space, a school of human diversity and a family for me. I had engendered and endowed a music so deep in me that I felt a radiant humanbeingness and charisma. Everyone who knew me understood exactly what I was doing. They loved me as much as I loved them. I had family at Pontiac Motors — and everywhere in Pontiac — who supported me and loved me for being myself.

I had some white friends at Pontiac Motors make bass bridges for me based on the ones I brought to them as a model, and they would make 4 or 5 new bridges in the wood shop department. I networked the Pontiac Motors Division. I went to a school with hundreds of skilled, very competent, scholars, builders, farmers, engineers, chemists, humanitarians, teachers, character builders, geniuses, chefs, connoisseurs of every description.

I was supported by people who gave me the full benefit of their strong and long support. I have to thank Dennis King, George Green, George "Red" Cotton, Laurie Sacks, Don Booth, Ralph Williamson, Jimmy King, Harry Albright, Tom Taylor, John Herring, Tom Andrew Ramsay, Larry Woods, Shine, Levi Jackson, Howard McCray. I can still tell you stories about my GM work family 30 years wide and deep.

Everyone left an indelible stamp on my psyche. Howard McCray came to hear me play and supported me like I supported him and his life. Several times, he, George Green, Art Hall, Roy Trevino, Pablo, Porter Williamson and countless others from my GM Motors family inspired me and respected me. They came to my house regularly, encouraged, pushed me and admired my epic ability to outlove them.

Many Friday nights Lofton Moran came to my house to bask in his seriousness. Lofton was from Florida and we were each both very serious about what we loved. I loved music and playing my music and he too loved music; and even though he did not play an instrument, he listened so seriously, it was as if he was playing right with us. He made you play hard by listening so hard and so seriously.

In September 1975, I entered Oakland Community College full time because Russ Grover, my supervisor insisted that I go to school. He said that I read too much not to be in school, so he almost literally pushed me through school doors and made certain my work schedule was tight. On school days on Tuesdays and Thursdays, I was given a two hour leeway. Instead of coming in at 2:30 pm, I could come in at 4:30 pm, and by 8:30 pm, I could study the night away.

In November, 1976 I transferred to the 11 - 7 midnight shift at Plant 2 Nickel Plating Corporation in Pontiac Motors, knowing that I would be working 7 days every week for two years on a special project of Buick Motors. Russ Grover was again my supervisor and he hooked up a schedule for me to come in at 1am and gave me two extra hours to play music on Friday nights. Russ Grover and I shared a very special bond, and I am so glad that he stayed on me, pushed , prodded and kept his faith in me.

I graduated from Oakland Community College with an associate degree in 1979 and from Oakland University with a degree in psychology and a minor in music and history. When I retired from Pontiac Motors in 1993, I immediately enrolled in graduate school in African American and African Studies and finished in 1996. General Motors paid my full school expenses.

ON FROM THE 70s INTO 2002

1976 saw me playing music from 8pm to 12 on Friday nights and on some Sundays and Saturdays during the early evenings. I worked 7 nights a week, went to school Monday, Tuesday, Wednesday and Thursday at O.C.C., and I locked into that time with relentless energy. I was drinking wheat germ, an organic juice tonic, a potion and an elixir and apple juice daily. I drank a quart jar every night at work and I became known for my health cleansing concoction.

Then, most significant was my addiction to Korean ginseng. I drank so much that I had to wean myself off of drinking so much. I cut down to just drinking my morning ounce on an empty stomach and gave up my ounce before bedtime; and I took one ounce before eating.

Ginseng gave me the energy to work at GM, go to school at O.C.C. and play Friday night music with energy, great strength and with a love that never dimmed or diminished.

At the same time I had powerful ongoing connections with a lot of penitentiary musicians and brothers who went to county jail, to Ionia, Marquette, Standish Maximum Correctional Facility and Jackson prison. Rashid and I always knew that the brothers in our generation in the 1960s were too set in their ways and would not be receptive at all to the music we were incessantly burning to play.

So, it is no wonder that all the musicians we recruited to play the music of the African Omnidevelopment Space Complex / We New came from the young street brothers, the brothers who went in and out of prison for years, the disenfranchised and the brigands who took the music played at my home inside the walls of many of Michigan's penal colonies.

One of the first two brothers that knew my music like he owned it is Donte Elliot. He lived right next door to me from 9 to 18, and his bedroom window stayed open in the hot summers and took all the nights the drums spoke to him to Ionia Correctional Facility for 11 long years.

In his letters to me, he remembered the musical outpouring that came from my house Friday in and Friday OUT. Donte ran in and out of my house when he was a child of N. Ardmore. He remembers how much music loved him. He absorbed the music in his cells, tissues, organs, brain, heart, bones and blood — and he lay deep in his cell and remembered the music so deep he could hear it.

Every Friday came so fast that it carried the weight of the day so swiftly that arrived in total cacophony of Friday night celebrations of music. Music ushered in the weekend and made the music be played harder, longer, higher and higher, and even as Donte was locked down in Ionia Correctional Facility, the music he had heard Friday night after Friday for years lived on in him.

Then one day after working all day in the kitchen, he came back to his cell to find that Melvin Hatchett was in a cell right next to him, and all the music he had heard at my house came full circle. In short, Melvin Hatchett had been one of the brothers who had regularly come to my house bringing his drums and had been one of the many drummers that Donte had listened to for years and years. Consequently they formed a transcendent band based on all the music Donte had heard and all the drums Melvin Hatchett had played. As a result, for years they kept the music alive in their many many talks and every Friday night they shared a connection from their prison cells with all the music that I continued to play. When they got out of Ionia, I was gratified to have them back with me musically and spiritually.

Moreover, a lot of brothers went to prison and came back home to find me still playing my music on into the 1980s, 1990s and up to 2002. There was Abdul Salaam, Jonathan Manning, Abdul Hamid, Michael Simpson, "Black" Bob Adams, William Myers, Jake Weathers, Kragin Bush, Butch Bard, Yusef Jones, Peter Jones, Mansu Abdul Hajj, Sadiq Goff, Muhammed Sekou Bey and others who spent time in the State of Michigan's correctional facilities and who also came home to find me still playing my music on Friday nights.

They all knew that I kept the music on fire while they were in their jail house beds and they all relished, revered and remembered the music I played. Of course, I wrote to them all and kept them abreast and aware of how the music was still a part of their lives no matter how long they were away.

Equally important, a lot of brothers moved to different parts of the world, such as patrick brennan, who moved to New York, and they all came back from time to time to play with me on Friday nights. Scott Pinkston moved to Norcross, Georgia, and he would bring his tenor and alto back every summer when he came come to visit his Pontiac family. Melvin Price made Sweden his home away from Pontiac, but he always came back with his trombone 2 or 3 times a year. Ted Russell found a job working in Muskegon, and he came down whenever he could with bass clarinet and kalimba. Fareed McKnight moved to Grand Rapids but remained devoted and dedicated to Pontiac Friday night music. Donald Washington took a job as a music teacher in Minnesota, and when school was out he brought all of his horns, tenor, alto, soprano, and baritone back to the Friday night music scene. When Joel Letvin had to move to West Bloomfield to be closer to his job, he made his clarinet playing presence felt every chance he could on Friday. Umam Saladuhim joined the army as a member of the 8th Army Band stationed in Germany. On leaves he always brought his bass clarinet, piccolo and flute back to the Friday night music sets. Andre Allen, tenor and alto, came back many Friday nights from Cleveland, Ohio after he got relocated to another GM plant. Todd Adams moved to Madison Heights but brought his piano straight to my house early on Friday so it would be on the set that night.

 I was so surprised at all the music played at my home and all the many musicians who loved playing with me. I have so many stories about all the wonderful music and wonderful musicians that honored me all the way up to year 2002. I am going to stop here in the 1970s to let everyone get a feel for the magnitude of the African Omnidevelopment Space Complex / We New Friday night music home concert series that I held up to 2002 in my home.

Afterword

1972 at the Ibo Cultural Center on 6 Mile Rd. near Woodward Avenue in Detroit, where all were awaiting a burn the house down performance by a McCoy Tyner Quartet that included Sonny Fortune, Alphonse Mouzon and Calvin Hill:

"Hey European Brother."

I had to do a double take. "Just what is he talking about? European? I'm not European. I don't get that. Okay, I'm American, okay ... but ... European?" I was thinking to myself. This wonderful, open hearted, generous person, had just sat down next to me and introduced himself as Ubadah Bey McConner (1937-2020), who eventually came to identify as Ra'maat Ubadah Hotep Ankh McConner Iheru.

Learning that I was an aspiring player, he immediately invited me to come up to a session at his place in Pontiac, an industrial city about 30 miles north of Detroit's central hub, and initiated a long lasting friendship that grew far closer to family depth than friendly acquaintance.

Being as inexperienced and naive as I was at the time, all of this seemed completely ordinary and natural to me, and it's the gift of a hindsight that's been able to perceive the cumulative ripple effect of these experiences that's allowed me to recognize just how extraordinary Ubadah's character, initiatives and achievements really are. In his own words, he has been living from the git-go a "charmed life" — a charmed condition of being that he's imparted to others whenever possible.

I'd been wondering if any press or scholars had ever documented and recognized the impact of The African Omnidevelopment Space Complex / We New, a home based cultural center that hosted an artist initiated musical situation in Pontiac for 3 decades from the early 70s into 2002, and I've come across no more than a short line or two in a small Pontiac paper. I've wondered why this has been so and have been considering the filters that so often define "history."

Conventional histories are, of course, told by those who've survived and even more so by those who happen to dominate. The reverse engineering of these "histories" tends to justify a status quo and to selectively construct a narrative that makes a particular version of the present seem inevitable.

In the case of most music histories, star status often decides the price of inclusion. And, just on the say so of succeeding generations of musicians who've adopted their influences, it's hard not to notice the impact of Armstrong, Ellington, Parker, Coleman and Coltrane. But, as the threads of affiliation have grown ever and more complex during the past 5 decades, attention has defaulted more to those who are most recorded, most written about and who manage to get paid to play overseas (and every so often, even right here in Gumboamerica).

Of course, musicians should be paid appropriately and enjoy some recognition, but this default position also instantly assumes that only market oriented career paths may yield "important" music and that the "serious" value of musical process derives only from its sonic product, whereas the reality of music is much more complex than this.

One of the many, many achievements of the A.A.C.M., for example, is that so many of its members both left Chicago and successfully engaged the international music market (and their musics merit that at the least). Although these successes have helped argue some credibility for their music, it still took an association member (and not an outside gatekeeper), George E. Lewis, to write and publish that group's history in "A Power Stronger than Itself."

But, what about other initiatives that stay local, don't even leave home and don't even address market relationships? Do these therefore "not exist" as "real" music? Are they only "amateur," "folk," "hobby," "amusement" or ... "therapy?" Imported classifications such as these sidestep and gloss over the actual complexity, range, variety and meaning of musical activity.

Ubadah, for his part, never waited for any outside permission to do what he wanted to do. He did it, documented it, mythologized and sustained it on his own terms, defining his own social and artistic aesthetics and standards while successfully working them through. He magnetized and thus drew the world in, rather than vice versa, continually keeping the process receptive to new musicians and new generations without preemptively locking into any single phase.

The intensity of his musical dedication and conviction nevertheless also radiated outwards, as musicians from all around the Detroit area were aware of what he was doing, with Faruq Z. Bey, Donald Washington and James Carter being among those who'd come through regularly.

The music has also concretely changed and redirected lives, where some grew into mature musicians. Others discovered alternatives to the undertow of the streets, while the music helped still others live and dream beyond the restrictions of their prison confinement.

I participated in activities at The African Omnidevelopment Space Complex / We New from 1972 till '75, when I drove with Sadiq, one of the drummers from that scene, to attempt for myself the artist and musician's life in NYC, and I've ever since felt myself an ambassador of the Space Complex. That world travels with me wherever I go.

Ubadah wholeheartedly accepted and encouraged anyone who came through his door, and this acceptance resonated with such a generosity that people would come to believe it — and even accept themselves more affirmatively in new ways. Such are the spaces he's created. The unconditional conviction with which he played also modeled how to do that oneself — and this is rarer than one might think.

Having since road tested my experiences with The Complex, I can attest to this contagion. When tactical and technical odds against my own artistic aspirations taste especially heavy, I notice that some of the unjustifiable confidence despite apparent evidence that sustains me is not just something I've cooked up on my own but draws also on the transcendent belief generated at 92 N. Ardmore.

This may not noticeably change the mad, probabilistic world we inhabit, but it can seriously alter what we choose to do with it. I don't think I'm at all the only participant, visitor or neighbor who's felt that way either. Just think about that Greek guy Archimedes' approach: "Give me a lever long enough and a fulcrum on which to place it, and I shall move the Earth."

- patrick brennan

www.ingramcontent.com/pod-product-compliance
Lightning Source LLC
Chambersburg PA
CBHW051701040426
42446CB00009B/1241